Porto Travel Guide 2023

The Insider's Complete Guide to Porto's Timeless Beauty, Unforgettable Experiences, and Must-See Attractions

Elaine P. Simmons

Table of Contents

+Bonus Section

- 20 special activities to engage in whenever you are in Porto
- Best places to eat
- Best Local Markets in Porto
- Best Vegetarian Restaurants in Porto
- Best Bars and Clubs in Porto
- Best Places For A Fancy Dinner In Porto

Introduction

Welcome to Porto, a city that perfectly encapsulates Portugal's illustrious past, thriving culture, and spectacular natural beauty. This Porto travel guide will take you on a discovery tour of a city full of hidden gems just waiting to be discovered as you flip the pages.

My name is [**Elaine P. S**], and I've had the good fortune to personally discover Porto's charm. Travelers from all over the world are drawn to Porto because of its distinctive Douro River, attractive alleys lined with colorful homes, and world-famous Port wine cellars.

When I first arrived in Porto, I was captivated by its distinctive fusion of medieval ambiance and modern dynamism. I was taken back in time as I strolled through the old Ribeira neighborhood, with its winding streets and charming squares, and I began to think about the generations who had lived here in the past.

I was in awe of the meticulous workmanship and the timeless beauty that grace Porto's streets thanks to the city's architectural wonders like the imposing Clérigos Tower and the charming Lello Bookstore. I was in awe of the layers of history that unfurled before my eyes as I explored the UNESCO World Heritage monuments, such as the Porto Cathedral and the city's medieval district.

Porto is a thriving center of culture in addition to being a city of historic treasures. I became engrossed in the vibrant art scene, learning about new galleries and street art that gave the city's design a contemporary edge. The lively festivities during festivals like So Joo and Santo António, the music-filled streets, and the beautiful melodies of Fado music all helped to capture the vibrant spirit of Porto and its voluminous cultural heritage.

Of course, no trip to Porto would be complete without enjoying some of its delectable cuisine. Porto's gourmet scene is a trip of tastes that pleased my taste buds and left me yearning for more. From traditional dishes like Francesinha and bacalhau to the world-famous Port wine and the exquisite pastéis de nata.

To provide you with the knowledge and resources to explore this interesting city with assurance and curiosity, I've created this Porto travel guide. Porto has something exceptional to offer everyone, whether they are history buffs, art connoisseurs, foodies, or just curious travelers.

So come along with me as we explore the city's hidden beauties, stroll through energetic districts, enjoy the flavors of Porto's food, and experience the friendliness and kindness of its residents. As you travel across the captivating city of Porto, let this guide be your traveling companion.

Prepare to be enthralled, moved, and transformed forever by Porto's beauty, allure, and spirit. Your adventure starts right here.

Chapter 1: Introducing Porto's Charm

Greetings from Porto: A Short Introduction

Welcome to Porto, a magical city where centuries of history and vivacious modernity coexist in perfect harmony. Porto, a city tucked away along the banks of the Douro River, captures the attention of everyone who visits. Porto provides a one-of-a-kind and amazing travel experience, from its stunning landscapes to its kind and welcoming people.

The Profound Past of Porto

Your entrance into Porto will seem like a step back in time. With a more than 2,000-year history, Porto is rich with magnificent treasures and interesting tales. Porto has experienced the rise and fall of empires, from its beginnings as a Roman town to its position as a successful trade port throughout the Age of Discovery. As a result, it has left behind a tapestry of historical landmarks and cultural riches.

Porto's Architectural Wonders: A Tour

Get ready to be in awe of Porto's architectural marvels as they line the city's streets. Romanesque, Gothic, Baroque, and

Neoclassical architectural styles are all represented throughout the city. Admire the elaborate facades of the famous Lello Bookstore and the Clérigos Tower, which served as models for J.K. Rowling's Harry Potter books. Get lost in the splendor of the So Bento Train Station, which is decorated with stunning azulejo tiles that feature historical images of Portugal.

Vibrant Porto Neighborhoods

The neighborhoods of Porto are a reflection of its vibrant character. Each area has its personality, from the ancient Ribeira district—a UNESCO World Heritage Site—to the hip Cedofeita and the creative feel of the Miguel Bombarda neighborhood. Discover the Miragaia's meandering, tiny alleyways and take in the quaint ambiance of Foz do Douro, where the river meets the Atlantic. Get to know the inhabitants in Bolho, a bustling market area, and discover what daily living is really like in Porto.

Porto's districts provide a complex tapestry of experiences, fusing heritage with modern flair, whether you're roaming through the ancient center of the city or strolling along the lively waterfront.

Prepare to be charmed as you travel across Porto by its fascinating history, breathtaking architecture, and lively districts. This is a city that begs you to wander around, get lost in its culture, and experience the friendliness of its residents. Prepare yourself to find hidden treasures, enjoy delectable meals, and make lifelong memories. Welcome to Porto, a remarkable location where charm and beauty converge.

Chapter 2: City Navigation

Getting Around: Porto's Transportation

Thanks to Porto's effective and extensive transit network, getting about the city is a snap. To meet the demands of every visitor, the city provides a variety of possibilities. Take a ride on one of the recognizable yellow trams that weave through the congested streets, offering a pleasant and nostalgic way to see the city. As an alternative, you can use Porto's large bus system to travel across the city and its surroundings. The metro system provides a dependable means to travel between the various regions of the city quickly and conveniently. Walking is a great opportunity to take in the ambiance and explore Porto's hidden gems at your own time if you prefer a more leisurely pace.

Travelers' Essential Portuguese Phrases

Learn a few basic Portuguese words to better integrate yourself into the community. Although English is widely spoken in Porto, making an effort to speak Portuguese will surely improve your experience and help you connect with the welcoming inhabitants. Learn basic salutations like "Bom dia" (Good morning), "Obrigado/a" (Thank you), and "Por favor" (Please). Use words like "Eu gostaria de um prato de Francesinha, por favor" (I would like a plate of Francesinha, please) to practice ordering your preferred regional meal. A few basic words may go a long way toward overcoming the language gap and demonstrating your respect for the regional norms.

Weather & When to Visit Porto Best

Porto is a year-round attraction because of its moderate and temperate environment. The typical summertime temperature is a comfortable 25 degrees Celsius (77 degrees Fahrenheit). When compared to other seasons, spring and fall are the best for seeing the city's outdoor attractions because of the warm weather and fewer crowds. Although the winters are mild, they can occasionally be wet, so make sure to bring an umbrella. Plan your trip to Porto during the famed So Joo Festival in late June, when the city comes alive with music, fireworks, and street parties, if you want to experience the city's dynamic atmosphere at its height.

Tips for Travelers' Safety

Although Porto is a typically secure city for visitors, it's always advisable to take security measures to guarantee a pleasant and worry-free journey. Be watchful about your possessions, especially while using public transit and in busy places. Keep valuable jewelry and huge sums of money out of sight. Like in any other city, it is best to stay in crowded, well-lit areas at night. Learn the emergency numbers and the location of the hospital or police station closest to you.

Finally, during your trip, trust your gut and use common sense.

Allow Porto's effective public transit system to take you to the city's intriguing sights as you navigate the city's lovely streets. Learn a few Portuguese words and watch as doors to a world of cultural immersion open up when you interact with the locals. To get the most out of your trip to Porto, plan your vacation around the festivities and weather. Above all, be careful and confident while you tour the city; Porto will welcome you with open arms.

Chapter 3: Taste of Porto

Foodie Delights: Porto's Restaurant Scene

Get ready to explore Porto's gastronomic treasures with your taste senses. The city is well known for its culinary culture, which offers a diverse array of sensations that will leave you wanting more. Every appetite will be satisfied in Porto, which offers everything from substantial traditional delicacies to cutting-edge modern food. Enjoy wonderful seafood dishes like grilled sardines and fresh octopus, or indulge at the famed Francesinha, a tasty sandwich with layers of ham, beef, and melting cheese. Don't forget to enjoy a glass of the best Porto wine with your dinner to enhance the dining experience with its distinctive characteristics.

The Renowned Porto Wine and Port Cellars

Without experiencing Porto's renowned wines, no trip there is complete. The famous Port wine, a sweet fortified wine that has been made in the area for generations, was first created in Porto. Explore the ancient cellars at Vila Nova de Gaia, which is close to the river, to learn the processes involved in making port wine. You may learn about the maturing process on a guided tour, go through huge basements filled with oak barrels, and partake in a tasting session where you can sample the various variations of this renowned wine. It's a chance to increase your enjoyment of this popular beverage and learn more about the skill that went into making it.

The Top Traditional Recipes

Embrace Porto's delights by savoring some of its traditional must-have meals. Start your gastronomic journey with a cup of the nourishing soup Caldo Verde, which is prepared with kale, potatoes, and chorizo. A traditional Portuguese meal made with salted codfish, potatoes, onions, and olives is called Bacalhau à Gomes de Sá. It is tasty and soft. The flavorful and tender Cozido à Portuguesa, a substantial meat and vegetable stew, is a real treat for meat lovers. Of course, don't forget to indulge in delectable sweet delicacies like the creamy custard pastry Pastel de Nata and the seductive scent of freshly baked Po de Ló, a soft sponge cake.

Local Food Markets and Cafés are Hidden Gems

Go off the beaten track to find Porto's hidden jewels if you want to taste the city's gastronomic spirit in its purest form. Discover the Mercado do Bolhao, a lively traditional food market with vibrant kiosks selling fresh vegetables, flavorful spices, and regional specialties. Talk to the welcoming merchants and try some local delicacies. Enter one of Porto's quaint cafés for a comfortable and genuine café experience, like Café Majestic, a wonderfully maintained Art Nouveau jewel that has been serving delectable pastries and fragrant coffee since 1921. You may establish a connection with the regional culinary tradition and make lifelong memories at these hidden jewels.

As you experience Porto's culinary scene, let the city's delicacies entice your palate. Enjoy regional cuisine's rich culinary heritage by sampling traditional dishes. Explore the world of Porto wine and learn about the centuries-old customs that go into its creation. Engage with the locals at restaurants and food markets to fully experience Porto's thriving culinary scene. Let your senses lead you on this culinary journey, and be ready to be astounded by the mouthwatering flavors that await you in this gourmet haven.

Chapter 4: Eye-Catching Sights

Exploring the UNESCO World Heritage Sites in Porto

Discover Porto's UNESCO World Heritage Sites, evidence of the city's rich history and magnificent architecture, and get ready to be amazed. The Ribeira District is a UNESCO-listed treasure that takes you back in time with its vibrant structures surrounding the Douro River. Take a stroll along the waterfront to enjoy the quaint ambiance and the historic structures that highlight Porto's nautical history. The old core of Porto, another UNESCO site worth seeing, is home to architectural marvels like the So Bento Train Station, which is covered in stunning azulejo tiles portraying moments in Portuguese history. These locations, which highlight Porto's cultural and historical importance, are a veritable visual feast.

Ribeira District Touring the Historic Center

Wander around the fascinating Ribeira District to enter the heart of Porto's past. Get lost in the maze-like streets that are ornamented with vibrant facades and flower-filled balconies.

Enjoy a stroll along the riverfront promenade while taking in the stunning scenery and the majestic Dom Luis I Bridge. Discover hidden jewels by exploring the little lanes, including beautiful neighborhood stores and authentic restaurants selling mouthwatering Porto wine. Don't pass up the chance to have a delicious lunch at one of the riverfront eateries while taking in the atmosphere and the breathtaking view of the Douro River. The Ribeira District is a veritable treasure mine of history, culture, and natural beauty.

Architectural Gems: Clérigos Tower and Lello Bookstore

Be ready to be in awe of Porto's skyline's architectural splendor. A recognizable landmark of the city that gives sweeping vistas of Porto is the Clérigos Tower. As you make your way up the tower's steep stairway, stop to take in the amazing views that span as far as the eye can see. The Lello Bookstore, a veritable haven for book lovers and a source of inspiration for J.K. Rowling is another architectural marvel not to be missed. Take in the fascinating atmosphere of the bookstore with its beautifully carved oak bookcases and grand staircase in the middle that appears to take you elsewhere. You will be in awe of these architectural wonders, which are a tribute to Porto's rich cultural legacy.

Other Iconic Landmarks Include the Majestic Café

At the Majestic Café, a famed Porto institution that has been serving residents and tourists since 1921, you may enter a world of luxury and old-world charm. With its elaborate façade and sumptuous interior, this beautiful café is a gem of Art Nouveau architecture. Enjoy one of their mouth-watering pastries or a cup of their scented coffee while taking in the café's historic setting. Other famous sites in Porto may be explored in addition to the Majestic Café. These sites provide a window into Porto's illustrious past and architectural variety, from the magnificent Palácio da Bolsa, a neoclassical masterpiece, to the enormous Avenida dos Aliados, the city's major thoroughfare lined with exquisite buildings and humming with activity.

Explore the alluring attractions of Porto as you set off on a quest of exploration. Take in the history and culture that are alive at the UNESCO World Heritage Sites. Peruse the charming and alluring Ribeira District as you stroll along the river. Admire the Clérigos Tower and the Lello Bookstore, two architectural wonders where inspiration and beauty meet. Enjoy the Majestic Café's opulent atmosphere while learning about other famous sites that highlight Porto's grandeur. Let your imagination go wild and your respect for the city's rich history grow with each sight you take in. You may be sure that Porto's stunning views will make a lasting impression on your trip.

Chapter 5: Experiencing Porto's Culture

Porto's Art Scene: Galleries and Museums

Get lost in the bustling art culture of Porto, a place that exudes inspiration and creativity. Explore the many galleries and museums that present a wide variety of artistic expressions. Visit the Serralves Museum to view provocative exhibitions and installations. This modern art museum is situated within a beautiful park. Explore the Fundação de Serralves, which houses a sizable collection of contemporary treasures, to learn more about Portuguese contemporary art. Explore the lovely galleries in the Miguel Bombarda neighborhood for a more personal art experience, where regional artists exhibit their creations in unique settings. Whether you enjoy contemporary or traditional art, Porto's art scene provides an enthralling voyage into imagination and creativity.

Fado Music: Porto's Soulful Melodies

Experience one of Portugal's most recognizable cultural traditions while listening to the soul-stirring sounds of Fado music. Fado, which is Portuguese for "fate" or "destiny," is a kind of music that perfectly captures the morose nature of Portuguese culture. Intimate settings in Porto allow you to experience the raw emotional power of fado performances. Fado singers' evocative vocals may be heard as they convey the pleasures and tragedies of life while being backed by the strums of guitars. Accept the depth of feelings that Fado inspires and let the music carry you away to a realm of desire and melancholy.

Festivals and Events Celebrated in Porto

Porto is a city that knows how to have a good time, and its festivals and events provide visitors with a look at the thriving local way of life. Participate in the festive atmosphere of Porto's midsummer festival, the So Joo Festival, which features music, dancing, fireworks, and street parties. Discover the magic of Christmas in Porto as the city is illuminated by holiday decorations and local markets. Attend events like the Festa do So Bento da Porta Aberta, a religious pilgrimage that commemorates Porto's patron saint, to fully immerse yourself in the city's cultural history. Every festival and event offers a chance to get to know the locals, experience Portuguese customs directly, and make lifelong memories.

Accepting Portuguese Customs and Traditions

Accept the rich tapestry of Portuguese traditions and practices to appreciate Porto's culture to its fullest. Enjoy the warm welcome you receive from the people as they invite you into their homes and hearts. Enjoy the laid-back Portuguese way of life by having vibrant discussions over a cup of coffee or a bottle of Port wine. Taste traditional fare and treats like the renowned Pastel de Nata or the cherished Francesinha, and take in the flavors that make Portuguese cuisine unique. Engage in age-old traditions by taking part in community celebrations or learning how to make traditional crafts. You'll develop a stronger bond with Porto's culture and residents if you embrace Portuguese traditions and practices.

Explore Porto's vibrant art scene, lose yourself in the eerie sounds of fado, and join the people in celebrating during festivals and events to fully immerse yourself in the city's rich cultural tapestry. You may truly experience Porto's culture and make memories that will last long after your trip by adopting Portuguese traditions and customs. As you explore the beauty and complexity of this enchanting city, let Porto's rich and varied cultural offerings inspire and enrich your journey.

Chapter 6: Outdoor Adventures

Gorgeous Beaches Close to Porto

Escape the hustle and bustle of the city and explore the breathtaking beaches close to Porto, where the sun, sand, and sea combine to create a tranquil and scenic environment. The golden sands of Matosinhos Beach are only a short distance from the city center, making them ideal for a stroll or a cool swim in the Atlantic. Visit the picturesque coastal town of Espinho, which is renowned for its outstanding surfing conditions and lively atmosphere, for a more isolated and wild experience. Discover Vila do Conde's unspoiled beauty, where beautiful beaches extend as far as the eye can see and beckon you to unwind. These lovely beaches provide an exquisite retreat where you can get in touch with nature and enjoy the peace of Porto's coastal attractions.

A Beautiful Adventure: Douro River Cruise

Take a leisurely journey down the Douro River and see the breathtaking scenery that will be shown to you. Take a tour of the Douro Valley, which is known for its terraced vineyards and quaint riverbank villages and is a UNESCO World Heritage Site. As you cruise by charming vineyards and quintas, take in the breathtaking views of green hillsides studded with rows of grapevines. Admire the gorgeous river bridges' exquisite architecture, including Porto's renowned Dom Luis I Bridge. Discover the tranquility of the Douro River and the natural beauty and rich cultural history that surround this magnificent waterway.

Visiting Porto's Parks and Gardens

Discover Porto's secret green oasis as you tour the city's gardens and parks, where the beauty of nature thrives. On a hilltop, Jardins do Palácio de Cristal offers stunning views of the city and is home to well-kept gardens, enchanting fountains, and romantic walks. Take a stroll around the quiet Parque da Cidade, Portugal's largest urban park, with its verdant landscape, twisting paths, and serene lakes. Visit the charming and entrancing Jardim das Virtudes, a park with sweeping views of the Douro River, to escape the bustle of the city. These lush getaways offer a tranquil haven, enabling you to get in touch with nature and find comfort in Porto's natural settings.

Stunning Douro Valley Day Trips

Take a day excursion to the magnificent Douro Valley, a refuge of natural beauty and a haven for wine lovers. You may reach this gorgeous area, typified by terraced vineyards, quaint villages, and rolling hills, by a leisurely journey from Porto. Visit Quintas (wine estates) and partake in wine tastings to experience the famed Douro wines' tastes and scents firsthand. As you travel the meandering roads that meander beside the river and provide picture-perfect vistas at every bend, take in the breathtaking scenery. Discover the timeless ambiance of Pinho and Peso da Régua's historic villages as you immerse yourself in the area's rich cultural history. A day excursion to the Douro Valley is a once-in-a-lifetime opportunity to see the beauty of nature and the fine skill of winemaking in a setting that is quite magnificent.

Explore Porto's serene gardens and parks, take a boat along the picturesque Douro River, go on day tours to the mesmerizing Douro Valley, and more to learn about the natural beauties that surround the city. These outdoor getaways provide you with the chance to relax, get in touch with nature, and revitalize your spirit. Accept the splendor of Porto's natural surroundings, and let the serenity of the outdoors motivate and inspire you while you go.

Chapter 7: A Merchandise Paradise

Porto's Shopping Avenues and Neighborhoods

Prepare to indulge in some retail therapy as you peruse Porto's thriving shopping district. The city has a wide selection of retail avenues and areas where you may get anything from high-end clothing to distinctive handcrafted goods. The main street of Porto, Avenida dos Aliados, is lined with chic boutiques and department stores that are ideal for those who love fashion and luxury. The Rua de Cedofeita has independent shops and hip concept stores for a more eclectic and bohemian shopping experience. An active retail district, Rua Santa Catarina mixes well-known worldwide brands with regional favorites to provide a wide selection of goods for all price ranges. Discover the ideal souvenirs by exploring these shopping areas, each of which has its character.

Traditional Crafts and Original Souvenirs

Immerse yourself in Porto's illustrious creative history and take home one-of-a-kind trinkets and local handicrafts as keepsakes of your trip. Visit the stores and ateliers that display the work of regional craftsmen. You may discover a broad variety of traditional crafts that represent Porto's cultural identity, from hand-painted azulejo tiles to finely woven fabrics. Look for Vila Nova de Gaia's traditional pottery, which is renowned for its delicate patterns and brilliant colors. Learn about the filigree craft, where talented artists use sophisticated metalworking methods to produce magnificent jewelry. You may assist regional artists while also bringing a bit of Porto's creative legacy into your own life by selecting these distinctive mementos.

Fashion in Porto: Stores and Designers

Enter the world of Porto's fashion industry, where innovation and style meet. The city is home to several up-and-coming designers and independent stores that provide a novel perspective on fashion. Learn about emerging Portuguese designers who display their expertise in exquisitely designed stores. You may choose from a wide variety of styles that appeal to every taste, from cutting-edge creations to timeless classics. Explore Porto's quaint side alleyways to find hidden treasures that provide one-of-a-kind apparel, accessories, and jewelry. Immerse yourself in Porto's fashion scene, and take advantage of the chance to find intriguing new looks for your wardrobe.

Finding Hidden Treasures in Vintage and Flea Markets

Find unique items and buried treasures at Porto's vintage and flea markets, where the past comes to life. Visit the Feira da Vandoma, a well-known flea market open every Saturday, where you can peruse a wide selection of stalls selling retro apparel, vintage furnishings, and unique treasures. Explore the Mercado do Porto Belo's maze to lose yourself in the unusual mix of old clothing, vinyl records, and sentimental mementos. These markets provide a treasure trove of one-of-a-kind things as well as the chance to learn untold tales about Porto's past. As you explore these historic havens, follow your curiosity; you never know when you'll find a real gem.

Start your shopping journey in Porto, a haven for people looking for a variety of retail experiences. Discover a variety of alternatives for every taste and budget as you explore the city's retail streets and neighborhoods. Find one-of-a-kind trinkets and regional handicrafts to support regional craftspeople and carry a bit of Porto's cultural legacy back home. Explore the city's fashion industry in-depth to find up-and-coming designers and boutique finds that will give your wardrobe some flair. Find hidden gems in antique and flea markets, where artifacts from the past come to life and each one has a tale to tell. Experience excitement, inspiration, and the delight of finding something unique during your shopping trip in Porto.

Chapter 8: Entertainment and Nightlife

The Exciting Nightlife in Porto: Bars and Clubs

When the sun goes down, Porto comes to life with a booming nightlife. Get ready to be completely consumed by the vigor and excitement of the city's pubs and clubs. Porto provides a wide variety of alternatives to suit every taste, from hip cocktail lounges to energetic music venues. Discover the lively streets of the Ribeira neighborhood, where quaint bars and patios overlook the Douro River and provide the ideal ambiance for a night of leisure and socialization. Immerse yourself in the vibrant atmosphere of the Galerias de Paris street, which is renowned for its varied mix of pubs and clubs that attract a diverse population. Experience the pulsing heartbeat of Porto's nightlife as you dance the night away to a range of musical styles, from electronic rhythms to live bands.

Concerts & Live Music Venues in Porto

Porto is a mecca for spectacular live performances and concerts for music lovers. Explore the city's quaint live music venues to learn more about its thriving music culture. Casa da Msica, a masterpiece of architecture devoted to music, presents a wide variety of acts, from classical concerts to shows including modern music. Coliseu do Porto is a beautiful historical arena that hosts world-famous musicians for spectacular performances. Explore the city's little taverns and cafés that provide live music for a more private experience, where you may sip a beverage and take in the melodies of skilled local musicians. Let Porto's live music scene infuse your spirit with rhythm and melody while you make lifelong memories.

Traditional Wine Bars and Tascas

Enjoy the unique flavors of Porto by immersing yourself in the original atmosphere of classic Tascas and wine bars. Tascas are modest, homey restaurants that serve substantial, delectable Portuguese cuisine. Enjoy classic Petiscos (small dishes) with regional wines or crisp beers. Discover the residents' favorite Tascas by exploring the city's secret areas. These places have a fun atmosphere and delicious cuisine. Wine lovers may choose from a variety of Portuguese wines, including the well-known Port wine, in Porto's wine bars. Enjoy a drink of your preferred vintage or go on a wine-tasting excursion with the assistance of professional sommeliers who will help you understand the subtleties of Portuguese wines. The culinary and wine culture of Porto is authentically and completely experienced at these classic tascas and wine bars.

Theater and Cultural Performances

Attend enthralling events and theatrical productions to immerse yourself in Porto's rich cultural tapestry. There are several theaters and cultural centers in the city that host a wide range of activities, including theatrical shows, dance recitals, and even circus acts. Visit the Teatro Nacional So Joo, a historic theater that offers a variety of plays and shows, from the classical to the modern. At the Rivoli Theater, a cutting-edge location that regularly presents a variety of cultural events, immerse yourself in the world of performing arts. You will be transported to a world of invention and imagination by Porto's cultural productions, which range from thought-provoking plays to hypnotic ballet performances.

Allow Porto's thriving nightlife and entertainment scene to enthrall you as the sun sets. Discover the city's pubs and clubs while dancing to the music's beats and soaking in the nightlife. Visit the live music venues to discover how songs come to life and produce amazing moments. Enjoy the genuineness of traditional tascas and wine bars while delighting in regional delicacies and absorbing the spirit of Porto's cuisine. Explore the realm of performing arts and cultural events, and let Porto's artists' talent and ingenuity move and inspire you. Allow Porto's nightlife and entertainment to enliven your soul and leave you with lifelong memories.

Chapter 9: Activities That Are Family-Friendly

Porto for Kids: Parks and Museums

Families are welcome in Porto, which provides a variety of fun activities for children of all ages. Explore the kid-friendly museums in the city, such as the World of Discoveries, where immersive experiences and interactive displays transport you to Portugal's Age of Exploration. The antiques and exhibits in the Museu da Cidade provide a fascinating look into Porto's past. Children may run, play, and enjoy the playgrounds and open spaces in Porto's largest urban park, Parque da Cidade, for outdoor experiences. Discover Porto's family-friendly attractions, which will stimulate young brains with unforgettable experiences.

Adventures that are Fun: Amusement Parks

Entertainment and excitement are assured in Porto's theme parks as you set out on fun-filled excursions. Visit SEA LIFE Porto, an aquarium that allows youngsters to interact with marine life while also learning about it. Children may have a lot of fun on various rides, games, and play areas at Funny City, an indoor amusement park, where they can occupy themselves for hours on end. The adjacent park of Magikland provides a superb selection of heart-pounding thrills for people looking for thrilling rides and attractions. Let your kids experience the fun and wonder that Porto's theme parks have to offer, and watch as they make priceless memories of laughing and excitement.

Family-friendly Cafes and Restaurants

Enjoy delectable food while making sure your eating experience in Porto is family-friendly. There are several family-friendly eateries and coffee shops in the city that provide kid-friendly menus and inviting environments. Find quaint coffee shops where you can take your time enjoying a leisurely breakfast or afternoon snack while indulging in delicious pastries and scented coffees. Discover family-friendly eateries that provide a variety of foreign and Portuguese meals to satisfy even the pickiest diners. Parents may unwind while their children are amused at certain restaurants that even offer special play spaces or activities for kids. Discover the welcoming atmosphere of Porto's family-friendly restaurants, where delectable cuisine and pleasant memories are assured.

Exploration and Outdoor Recreation

The outdoor areas of Porto provide countless chances for family exploration and excursions. Enjoy a stroll along the beautiful Douro River while taking in the vibrant Ribeira neighborhood and the famous bridges that cross the river. Discover the Crystal Palace's magnificent gardens, where kids may play on the playgrounds and run around unrestrained among the rich vegetation. Explore the Douro Valley's breathtaking scenery outside of the city boundaries or the adjacent beaches for family-friendly outdoor activities like picnics, beach games, and even water sports. Allow Porto's magnificent outdoors to serve as your playground as you inspire in your kids a feeling of awe and a love of the natural world.

There are many family-friendly activities in Porto that appeal to both young and old. Discover the fascinating parks and museums that capture children's attention and pique their interest. Adventures filled with joy and excitement may be had in theme parks. Enjoy delectable meals at family-friendly eateries to make sure that everyone has a special eating experience. Take part in outdoor pursuits and exploration to connect with nature as a family and make lifelong memories. Embrace Porto's kind attitude toward families and go out with your loved ones on a memorable adventure filled with joy and discovery.

Chapter 10: Recreation and Sports

Porto's Sporting Heritage: Football and Other Sports

Immerse yourself in Porto's rich athletic history, a city renowned for its love of football and many other sports. Visit FC Porto, one of Portugal's most storied football clubs, and take in a game at the magnificent Estádio do Drago. Experience the excitement of the audience as they support their team, making for an exciting athletic event. Porto also has a variety of other sports to enjoy besides football. At the city's sports facilities, play a friendly game of basketball, volleyball, or handball or experience the excitement of a rugby or basketball contest. Take part in Porto's athletic culture and be motivated by the athletes' and supporters' zeal.

Outdoor Activities and Water Sports

Take advantage of Porto's seaside position by participating in a range of thrilling outdoor activities and water sports. Surfing, stand-up paddleboarding, and kayaking are just a few of the sports you may use to explore the breathtaking Atlantic coastline. Catch a wave or negotiate the calm Douro River waters to experience exhilaration. Enjoy a leisurely boat ride around the river, taking in the magnificent sights of Porto's shoreline, for those looking for a more laid-back experience. The parks and green areas of the city also provide chances for outdoor pursuits like running, cycling, or just taking a leisurely picnic in the middle of nature. Explore Porto's natural playground and let your daring side go.

Tennis Courts and Golf Courses in Porto

Porto has top-notch facilities and courses for tennis and golf players of all ability levels. Start your round at one of Porto's world-class golf courses, such as Oporto Golf Club or Miramar Golf Club, to experience a demanding game amidst picturesque scenery and breathtaking coastline vistas. At one of the city's tennis clubs, you may sharpen your serve or take part in a friendly match while enjoying the well-kept courts and qualified instruction. Whether you're an expert golfer or a beginner at tennis, Porto offers the ideal atmosphere for you to enjoy your favorite sports and improve your abilities.

Centers for Wellness and Fitness

At Porto's fitness and wellness facilities, keep up your exercise program and give your health priority. Find cutting-edge gyms with cutting-edge equipment where you can participate in a range of training courses or work out at your speed. Attend yoga or Pilates classes that encourage balance and relaxation to find your zen. Utilize wellness therapies and spa services to relax and refresh your body and mind. The fitness and wellness facilities in Porto provide a comprehensive approach to health, giving you the instruments and materials you need to reach your fitness objectives and foster a sense of well-being.

Embrace Porto's sports and leisure scene, where a variety of events are waiting to revitalize your body and spirit. Experience the passion of football and learn about other exhilarating sports as you get fully immersed in the city's athletic history. Take part in outdoor activities and water sports that will let you connect with Porto's stunning natural environment. Start your round at world-class golf courses or hone your serve at tennis clubs. Put your health and fitness first at modern fitness and wellness facilities. In Porto, where sports and recreation form an essential part of your trip, embrace an active and balanced lifestyle.

Chapter 11: Discovering Porto's Secrets

Off the Beaten Track: Porto's Undiscovered Gems

Explore Porto's hidden gems, where the city's mysteries and lesser-known treasures are waiting, by veering off the beaten route. Discover the Miragaia neighborhood's small alleys, vibrant homes, and scenic riverbank as you explore this lovely area hidden from the busy tourist areas. Find the Fonte da Virtude, a peaceful corner fountain where people have long had a belief in the therapeutic properties of its waters. Explore the Mercado Bom Sucesso, a bustling food market popular with residents but sometimes overlooked by tourists, where you can try local specialties and take in the energetic environment. You may discover a real, unanticipated, and delightfully surprising side of Porto by stepping outside the usual tourist destinations.

Legends & Ghost Stories from Mysterious Porto

Discover the spooky and enigmatic stories that have permeated Porto's past. Porto is a city with a rich tapestry of folklore and unexplained stories, from haunted homes to ghostly apparitions. Discover the notorious "House of Seven Bats" in Rua do Reboleira, which is rumored to be haunted by paranormal activity. Learn about the spooky lore surrounding the Lello Bookstore and the paranormal nuns who are said to haunt the Carmo Church. Join a ghost tour or just take a nighttime stroll around Porto's winding lanes, letting the city's eerie ambiance capture your imagination. The interesting layer of magic that Porto's ghost stories add to its already alluring environment.

Street Art in Cities and Alternative Cultures

Explore Porto's thriving urban street art culture, where originality and self-expression are prioritized. Explore Porto's streets to see fascinating murals, provocative graffiti, and breathtaking art installations. Discover the city's creative center, the Rua Miguel Bombarda, where independent art galleries and innovative exhibition venues present modern artworks. Participate in Porto's thriving alternative culture by going to poetry readings, experimental theater productions, or underground music shows. Let Porto's alternative culture and street art serve as an inspiration for your artistic endeavors.

Undiscovered Communities and Weird Attractions

Explore Porto's unknown districts and oddball sights as you set out on a voyage of discovery. Visit Foz do Douro, a little coastal community with opulent houses and lovely beaches that offers a tranquil and relaxed atmosphere. Discover the

Parque de Serralves, a magnificent green oasis with beautiful gardens and a museum of modern art that offers a calm haven from the bustle of the city. Seek out eccentric attractions where you may test your problem-solving abilities in an immersive journey, like Livraria Lello's secret staircase or the fascinating Puzzle Room. Explore Porto's unexplored areas and oddball attractions, and let your curiosity lead you to memorable encounters and undiscovered gems.

Discover hidden treasures that reveal Porto's genuine spirit when you stray from the usual route and uncover the city's mysteries. Become engrossed in the eerie mythology and ghost stories that surround Porto with a sense of mystery. Engage in the alternative culture and thriving urban street art scene that gives the city's buildings and underground venues life. Set off on explorations into uncharted districts and look for oddities that will surprise you along the way. You may establish a stronger connection with the city, its legends, and its distinctive personality by learning Porto's secrets.

Chapter 12: Planning Day Trips

Aveiro, the Venice of Portugal, is a Day Trip Away.

Take a day trip to Aveiro, sometimes known as the "Venice of Portugal," to see its distinct charm and picture-perfect canals. Glide over the tranquil canals in a Moliceiro, a traditional boat decorated with bright colors and elaborate ornaments, and discover the city. Admire the beautiful art nouveau structures that border the canals, which serve as a reminder of a more opulent and beautiful time. Enjoy delectable local treats called Ovos moles while strolling along the Ria de Aveiro, a lagoon that spans along the coast. Aveiro is the ideal location for a tranquil and alluring day excursion because of its beautiful ambiance and charming streets.

Guimares and Braga: Historical Gems

Visit Braga and Guimares, two cities that had a big impact on Portugal's colorful past, to go on a historical adventure. As the "Rome of Portugal," Braga is home to an astounding number of sacred sites, including the breathtaking Bom Jesus do Monte sanctuary. Discover Braga's old center with its winding lanes, quaint squares, and lively atmosphere. Guimares, known as the birthplace of Portugal, provides a window into the history of the region. Explore the magnificent Guimaraes Castle, a UNESCO World Heritage Site, and take in the city's architectural splendor as you stroll through its medieval alleyways. These historical treasures offer an enthralling glimpse into Portugal's history and are likely to inspire you.

Matosinhos and Vila do Conde are Two Coastal Getaways.

Escape to the charming seaside communities of Matosinhos and Vila do Conde, where you can enjoy the area's fine beaches, delectable seafood, and laid-back atmosphere. Surfers and beach lovers flock to Matosinhos for its world-famous beaches. Enjoy delectable seafood at the nearby eateries, which are renowned for offering some of the freshest fish and shellfish in the area. Vila do Conde, with its lovely streets, scenic riverside, and ancient city center, provides a more serene beach experience. Visit the magnificent Vila do Conde Aqueduct, take in the tranquil beauty of the adjacent Póvoa de Varzim beach, and explore the town's medieval architecture. These seaside getaways provide the ideal blend of leisure and scenic beauty.

Entertaining Peneda-Gerês National Park

Take a trip to the captivating Peneda-Gerês National Park, a breathtaking natural paradise that fascinates with its biodiversity and gorgeous scenery. A tranquil and picturesque environment is created by flowing waterfalls and clear streams as you hike through the thick woodlands. Explore the untamed splendor of the highlands, which are studded with historic hamlets and granaries. Discover the vast network of paths in the park, which provide everything from easy strolls to strenuous treks, and you'll be rewarded with spectacular panoramic vistas. Take in the peace of the outdoors, inhale the clean mountain air, and let Peneda-Gerês National Park fill you with amazement and wonder.

Create your day trips from Porto and see the many beauties that are around. Discover the allure of Aveiro's canals, savor the history of Braga and Guimares, unwind in the seaside getaways of Matosinhos and Vila do Conde, and savor the enchantment of Peneda-Gerês National Park's stunning vistas. Each day's tour provides a different experience and an opportunity to see northern Portugal's natural beauty and cultural variety. Allow your travels outside of Porto to broaden your horizons and provide lifelong memories.

Chapter 13: Porto's Sustainable Tourism

Porto's Eco-Friendly Practices

Learn about the environmentally friendly initiatives that make Porto a city dedicated to sustainable tourism. Porto makes efforts to lessen its carbon footprint and support environmental preservation, including energy-efficient construction and renewable energy projects. Many lodgings in Porto place a high priority on sustainability by implementing eco-friendly methods including reducing trash, conserving electricity and water, and providing eco-friendly facilities. To reduce your carbon footprint, explore the city on foot, hire a bike, or take public transportation. Make ethical decisions while you are there to support Porto's sustainability initiatives and adopt the city's eco-conscious ethos.

Activities Related to Ecotourism and Green Spaces

Spend time in Porto's open spaces and take part in ecotourism activities that will help you connect with nature and promote environmental preservation. Visit the Parque da Cidade, a sizable urban park with verdant scenery, tranquil walks, and leisure spaces. Discover the magical gardens of Serralves Park, where art and nature coexist together. Visit the adjacent Peneda-Gerês National Park, which is home to a variety of ecosystems and breathtaking vistas, and partake in activities like birding, trekking, or nature photography. You aid in the preservation of these priceless settings by engaging in ecotourism activities and savoring Porto's natural beauty.

Promoting Regional Crafts and Communities

Support regional businesses and crafts in Porto to embrace the idea of sustainable tourism. Look for locally run establishments that sell genuine Portuguese goods and contribute to the community's economy. Learn about the cultural history that local craftsmen are preserving by exploring traditional handicrafts including ceramics, needlework, and cork goods. Participate in programs for community-based tourism that provide genuine experiences, such as tours led by local authorities or workshops where you may learn traditional crafts. You may assist maintain cultural traditions and the way of life of the people who call Porto home by supporting regional businesses and handicrafts.

Ethical Decisions and Responsive Eating

Enjoy Porto's culinary treats while making ethical eating decisions that support sustainable lifestyles. Choose eateries that emphasize fresh vegetables, locally produced products, and sustainable seafood alternatives. Discover the thriving food markets in Porto, such as Mercado do Bolhão o Mercado da Ribeira, to get fresh, regional goods and to help small-scale farmers and producers. Pick restaurants and other businesses that recycle and compost to reduce trash. Think about having a meal at a social company or a restaurant that promotes social issues and helps the communities in Porto. You can help create a more sustainable food system and support organizations that put a priority on the environment and social well-being by choosing ethically and sensibly when you eat in Porto.

When visiting Porto, adopt sustainable tourism practices to support the city's dedication to environmental preservation and responsible tourism. Take part in environmentally responsible activities, such as lowering your carbon footprint and promoting sustainable lodging. Spend time in Porto's parks and gardens and take part in ecotourism activities to learn about and save the environment. By purchasing genuine, regionally produced goods, you can help support local businesses and crafts. Make ethical and sustainable practices a priority when choosing where to eat. You can help protect Porto's natural and cultural legacy and have a positive influence on the city and its future by using sustainable tourism practices.

Chapter 14:
Budget-Friendly Porto
Exploration

Porto's Free and Cheap Attractions

Learn about the abundance of free and reasonably priced attractions that let you see Porto without breaking the bank. As you stroll through the old town, stop to see the famous Dom Luis I Bridge, which provides sweeping views of both the city and the Douro River. Discover the picturesque streets, vibrant buildings, and bustling ambiance of the Ribeira neighborhood. Enjoy the serenity of the cloister of the Porto Cathedral, a remarkable specimen of Romanesque architecture. Learn about the Jardins do Palácio de Cristal, a gorgeous park with lovely gardens, tranquil strolling pathways, and breathtaking vistas. Take advantage of Porto's free walking tours to learn more about the history and culture of the city from qualified guides. You may enjoy Porto's beauty without breaking the bank thanks to a variety of inexpensive and free attractions.

Affordable Restaurants and Street Food

Discover inexpensive restaurants and indulge in mouthwatering street cuisine to experience Porto's delicacies without breaking the bank. Learn about the city's traditional eateries, where you can savor filling and reasonably priced fare like the renowned francesinha sandwich or a classic Bacalhau dish. Investigate neighborhood markets like Mercado do Bolhao or Mercado da Ribeira where you may try local food, including fresh produce and cheeses, at a fair price. Find delectable goodies like Bifanas (pork sandwiches), pasteis de nata (custard tarts), and fresh seafood nibbles in Porto's thriving street food scene. You may indulge your appetite for food while keeping within your budget by seeking out low-cost restaurants and enjoying street cuisine.

Options for Cheap Accommodations

In Porto, you may find inexpensive lodging alternatives that yet offer comfort and convenience. Look for guesthouses, hostels, or inexpensive hotels that provide reasonable rates and the necessities. If you want to visit Porto's attractions quickly and for the least amount of money on transportation, think about staying in the city center or close to public transit. Consider renting an apartment or vacation home if you're traveling in a group or with family. These accommodations can be more affordable, provide more room, and allow you to cook. You may locate a cozy location to relax and rejuvenate without breaking the bank by looking into the variety of economical lodging alternatives in Porto.

Savings Advice and Offers

While visiting Porto, make the most of your money by adhering to budget-friendly advice and taking advantage of offers. Consider getting a Porto Card, which grants free or reduced entrance to several attractions and unrestricted use of citywide public transit. Take advantage of special weekday or Sunday entrance rates, or discounted entry hours, at museums and cultural institutions. Save money on transportation expenditures and enjoy the flexibility to explore the city on foot or by renting a bike while in Porto. Find inexpensive snacks and picnic materials from your neighborhood markets and grocery stores. In restaurants with great value, keep an eye out for special offers or lunch menus. You may maximize your budget while touring Porto by being wise and keeping a lookout for money-saving advice and discounts.

Utilize the city's free and inexpensive attractions to explore Porto's delights on a budget. Snack at affordable restaurants and enjoy the mouthwatering tastes of Porto's street cuisine. Find accommodations that are cozy and reasonable and match your needs. To stretch your budget as far as possible, use offers and money-saving strategies. By visiting Porto on a tight budget, you can experience the city's cuisine, culture, and history without breaking the bank, making for an amazing and invigorating experience.

Chapter 15: The Wine Route of Porto

Porto's Cellars Wine Tasting

In Porto's renowned cellars, where the city's extensive wine legacy is brought to life, go on a wine-tasting experience. Visit Vila Nova de Gaia's ancient Port wine cellars, which are conveniently situated across the Douro River from Porto's downtown. Explore the vaults and learn about the painstaking procedures used to produce this magnificent beverage as you delve into the centuries-old heritage of port wine manufacturing. Enjoy a variety of Port wines, from silky tawnies to opulent vintage reserves, while you engage your senses. Discover the rich flavor, intricate fragrances, and velvety texture that have made port wine so renowned across the world. Your entranceway to a world of sensory enjoyment and appreciation for this exceptional wine may be found in the Porto cellars.

The Douro Valley Wine Region: An Exploration

Take a trip outside of the city to the stunning Douro Valley, one of the oldest wine districts in the world and a UNESCO World Heritage Site. Find more about the terraced vineyards that line the slopes and weave a magnificent tapestry of green and gold. Discover the quaint winery communities that dot the countryside, each with its own special charm and winemaking traditions. Interact with regional winemakers to learn about their commitment to creating premium wines, such as the famed Douro DOC wines. Immerse yourself in the Douro Valley's splendor and let the region's breathtaking vistas and world-class wines seduce your senses.

Vineyard Visits and Wine Tours

Engage in wine tours and vineyard excursions to gain a thorough understanding of Porto's wine culture. Join a guided tour that takes you through the beautiful countryside and lets you see how wine is made from the vine to the bottle. Visit family-run vineyards to learn about the distinctive qualities of the local grape varietals. Here, generations of winemakers have honed their trade. Take a stroll around the vineyards, take in the earthy aromas, and get a sense of how labor-intensive the growing and harvesting of grapes is. Participate in tastings conducted by trained sommeliers to learn more about the wide variety of wines produced in the area. Let the wine excursions and vineyard visits deepen your appreciation for and understanding of Porto's winemaking heritage.

Wine Pairing Workshops and Experiences

Learn more about the harmonious matching of food and wine by participating in wine-pairing events and courses. Learn the skill of combining local treats like handmade cheeses, charcuterie, and delectable chocolates with Port wines. Participate in seminars run by knowledgeable sommeliers who will explain the basics of food and wine matching and lead you through the subtleties of wine tasting. Discover the varied qualities of port wine and how they improve and complement the tastes of various foods. As you explore the exquisite pairings and discover the secrets of the best wine and food pairings, let your taste buds serve as your guide.

Join the Porto wine trail to explore the enticing Douro Valley and the world of Port wines. Enjoy wine tastings while experiencing the varied aromas of Port wine in Vila Nova de Gaia's ancient cellars. Discover the beautiful wine towns and stunning terraced vineyards of the Douro Valley. Take part in wine tours and vineyard excursions to learn about the wine-making process and sample world-class wines. Enjoy wine-matching activities and workshops to learn the skill of blending wine and food deliciously. Allow Porto's wine route to serve as your entryway into the world of wine enjoyment and a fascinating tour of the tastes and customs of Portugal's wine culture.

Chapter 16: The View of a Photographer

The Best Instagrammable Places in Porto

Find Porto's most Instagrammable locations and use your camera to capture the city's beauty. Start your photography tour in the famous Ribeira neighborhood, known for its vibrant structures, winding lanes, and scenic shoreline. Photograph the magnificent Dom Luis I Bridge's panoramic background and ornate ironwork to capture the breathtaking perspective of Porto. Visit the Livraria Lello, a bookshop that will take you to a fantastical location with winding stairs and magnificent design. Discover the wacky streets, gorgeous homes, and river vistas of the Miragaia neighborhood. Look for undiscovered jewels where vivid colors and original compositions are waiting like the Mercado do Bolhão or the Jardins do Palácio de Cristal. Allow Porto's Instagrammable locations to spark your imagination and serve as inspiration for taking pictures that portray the character of the city.

Photographic Advice for Capturing Porto's Soul

Follow these crucial photography strategies to capture the spirit of Porto in your pictures. To make aesthetically appealing photographs, pay attention to composition and use leading lines, symmetry, and frame. Make use of natural light, particularly during the golden hour when the city is illuminated by its warm, mellow tones. Try out various viewpoints and angles, getting low or getting high to get interesting perspectives. Look for intriguing textures and features that reveal the history and culture of Porto. Wait for the ideal opportunity to capture the character and ambiance of a location by being attentive and patient. By keeping these photography suggestions in mind, you may improve your pictures and portray Porto in all its authentic glory.

Nighttime and Golden Hour Photography

Learn about the wonder of night photography while taking in Porto during the city's golden hour. immediately before or immediately after dawn or sunset, during the golden hour, the gentle, warm light creates a dreamy atmosphere and casts a lovely glow over the city. Utilize this lovely moment to take pictures of beautiful landscapes, architectural features, and cityscapes that are illuminated by a golden color. Accept the challenge of taking nighttime photos as the sun sets and the city lights up. Take pictures of the lively nightlife, the lit bridges, and the Douro River's reflections. Try using long exposures to produce hypnotic light trails and record the motion of the city. You might give your visual account of Porto a hint of enchantment and mystery by utilizing the golden hour and night photography.

Aerial and Water Photography Perspectives

Explore aerial and water photography in Porto to elevate your photos to new heights. Consider employing drones to photograph Porto from above or looking for vantage spots on higher ground to capture the city's distinctive topography. Capture the Douro River's winding course and the magnificent buildings that border its banks. Explore Porto's canals instead by taking pictures of reflections and the dynamic city's activity from a fresh angle. To get a good look at Porto's famous bridges, vibrant homes, and riverfront vistas, rent a boat or go on a river tour. Aerial and underwater photography gives a novel and distinctive method to capture Porto's beauty and offer a viewpoint that is certain to make an impact.

Take in Porto's splendor and use your camera to capture the soul of the city. Discover the city's hidden jewels and famous monuments as you explore its Instagrammable locations. To improve your photos and portray Porto's authentic character, use these photography suggestions. Utilize the appeal of night photography and the enchantment of the golden hour to create evocative, arresting photos. Explore aerial and underwater photographs to show off Porto's distinctive viewpoints. Allow your love of photography to lead you on a visual tour of Porto, capturing its allure, past, and spirit in each picture.

Chapter 17: Porto during Christmas

Porto's Christmas Celebrations

Discover Porto's Christmas charm as the city comes to life with joyous celebrations and entrancing decorations. Explore the city's streets lined with sparkling lights and elaborate Christmas decorations. Visit the famous Avenida dos Aliados to see the enchanting ambiance created by the towering Christmas tree and the seasonal market. Explore the many handcrafted goods, customary delicacies, and one-of-a-kind presents available at the Christmas markets that are sprinkled across the city. Enjoy the festive atmosphere as carolers fill the room with their melodious sounds. Don't pass up the chance to enjoy seasonal treats, such as Rabanadas (Portuguese French toast) and Bolo Rei (King's Cake). Allow the Christmas spirit of Porto to warm your heart and jot down priceless recollections.

The Santo António Festival: A Vibrant Custom

Participate in the lively Santo António Festival, which honors Porto's patron saint and features a dynamic exhibition of regional customs. Experience the colorful parades that feature dance, music, and traditional attire. Join the inhabitants of Miragaia as they honor Santo António with street celebrations, exciting processions, and mouthwatering food vendors. Observe the magnificent fireworks show that illuminates the night sky and provides an enchanted setting for the celebrations. Take in the happy mood as residents and guests alike gather to celebrate their heritage and show their affection for their hometown. The Santo António Festival offers a chance to appreciate Porto's diverse culture and communal spirit.

So Joo Festival: The Midsummer Party in Porto

Enjoy the So Joo Festival, Porto's most awaited summertime celebration that lights up the city with music, dancing, and fireworks. Participate in exciting street parties that light up the night with fun and celebration. Discover the fascinating custom of striking one other on the head with plastic hammers, a playful action said to fend off bad luck and spirits. Participate in the merry marches, as individuals of all ages parade through the streets while holding lit balloons and singing classic melodies. Prepare to be fascinated as the night progresses by the magnificent fireworks show that lights up the sky over the Douro River. The So Joo Festival offers a chance to openly revel in life and is a real representation of Porto's joie de vivre.

Carnival and Other Holiday Celebrations

Entertain the jubilant atmosphere of Porto's Carnival, when the city is transformed into a vivacious stage of colorful costumes, parades, and music. Participate in the energetic processions that fill the streets with singing and dancing while admiring the imaginative and artistic designs of the costumes and floats. Witness the infectious enthusiasm as residents and tourists join forces to joyfully and merrily celebrate Carnival. Porto holds several other celebratory occasions throughout the year, such as the Festas of So Bento da Vitória, a cultural festival with performances of music, drama, and dance. Check the city's schedule of events to learn about further exciting celebrations that highlight Porto's rich artistic and cultural legacy.

As the city celebrates several holidays throughout the year, feel the joy of Porto. Enjoy the enchanted holiday ambiance, complete with dazzling decorations and merry marketplaces. Participate in the vibrant traditions of the Santo António Festival and take in the vibrant So Joo Festival, which ushers in the summer. Discover additional joyous occasions that reflect Porto's artistic and cultural diversity as well as the vivid Carnival celebrations. Engage your senses in the festive atmosphere and take part in the joyful events that make Porto come alive.

Chapter 18: Visiting Porto's Neighborhoods

Vila Nova de Gaia: Beaches and Port Wine
Vila Nova de Gaia, which is located just over the river from Porto, welcomes visitors with its extensive history, lovely waterfront, and famed Port wine cellars. Exploring the cellars and partaking in wine tastings will take you on a discovery-filled adventure as you become familiar with the tastes and customs of this famous wine from across the world. Take in the sights of Porto's historic district as you stroll down the waterfront promenade while taking in the cooling sea wind. Visit Vila Nova de Gaia's stunning beaches, such as Praia de Lavadores and Praia de Canide, to unwind, swim, and enjoy the sunshine. Vila Nova de Gaia is the ideal complement to your trip to Porto since it combines history, wine culture, and seaside appeal.

Aveiro Lagoon and Costa Nova Exploration

Explore the picturesque Aveiro Lagoon and the quaint village of Costa Nova by traveling south of Porto. Join a boat excursion in the lagoon to see the tranquil surroundings, the rich fauna, and the classic Moliceiro boats that provide some color to the waterways. Admire Costa Nova's distinctive striped residences, which have evolved into the community's defining feature. Enjoy the seaside ambiance as you stroll along the sandy beaches and feel the smooth sand under your toes. Enjoy delectable seafood at nearby eateries, where you may sample the most recent Atlantic Ocean catches. You may escape the city to a serene and picturesque location like the Aveiro Lagoon or Costa Nova and take in the area's breathtaking scenery.

Castro Laboreiro: Nature and Ancient Ruins

To find Castro Laboreiro, a hidden treasure tucked away in the Peneda-Gerês National Park, head north of Porto. Discover the historic remains of Castro Laboreiro Castle, which are set on a hilltop and provide sweeping views of the surrounding area. Explore the little town, which is renowned for its quaint stone homes and rural ambiance. Enjoy the natural surroundings of the national park, which has rocky mountains, flowing waterfalls, and a variety of species. Hike the paths while taking in the tranquillity of the surroundings and the crisp mountain air. In the center of the national park, Castro Laboreiro offers a chance to get in touch with nature, learn about historical history, and go on exciting excursions.

Guimares and Braga in the Past

Find out more about Guimares and Braga's rich historical and cultural history, two cities that had a significant impact on the development of Portugal. Visit Guimares' magnificent Guimaraes Castle, which is regarded as the birthplace of the Portuguese country, and tour the city's well-preserved medieval core, a UNESCO World Heritage Site. Take a stroll around the old city's cobblestone lanes, which are dotted with charming homes and boutiques. Discover spectacular religious sites in Braga, the "Rome of Portugal," including the Bom Jesus do Monte sanctuary, which has elaborate Baroque architecture. Discover the busy city center's lovely squares, bustling marketplaces, and cozy cafés. A worthwhile day trip from Porto, Guimares, and Braga provides an enthralling look into the history, art, and architecture of Portugal.

Immerse yourself in Porto's diverse surroundings by learning about the port wine tradition and coastal charm of Vila Nova de Gaia, exploring the Aveiro Lagoon and Costa Nova's natural beauty, exploring the nature and ancient ruins of Castro Laboreiro, and learning about the rich historical and cultural heritage of Guimares and Braga. Your tour of the area will be richer and more varied because each place provides a distinctive experience. Extend your horizons, travel outside of Porto, and let the natural beauty and rich history of the area enthrall your senses and enrich your adventure.

Chapter 19: Porto for Lovers of Art and Design

Galleries and Exhibitions of Modern Art

Explore the galleries and shows to fully experience Porto's thriving contemporary art scene. In contemporary art galleries like the Serralves Museum of Contemporary Art, where thought-provoking shows display a wide range of artistic disciplines, discover the cutting-edge creations of regional and global artists. Visit Maus Hábitos, a venue for creative exhibitions, performances, and events that supports up-and-coming artists. Discover the Centro Português de Fotografia, an institution devoted to the photography medium, and let the inspiring images and stories that the skilled photographers have captured inspire you. Porto provides a plethora of options to interact with current creative expressions thanks to its broad and vibrant contemporary art scene.

Design Studios and Districts

Explore the thriving design studios and areas of Porto to learn more about the city's design sector. Learn about the Largo de So Domingos neighborhood, which is regarded as the city's design center and is home to a variety of design stores, studios, and creative spaces. Explore distinctive pieces of furniture, clothing, and home décor made by regional designers and learn about their creative processes. Discover the Bombarda neighborhood, where you can find unique design items and fashionable accessories in its eclectic mix of design stores, concept boutiques, and art galleries. Visit design studios that specialize in a variety of fields, such as graphic design, textiles, and ceramics, to see how traditional craftsmanship and modern aesthetics are combined. Design fans can find a wealth of unique and inspirational works in Porto's design studios and areas.

Graffiti Fours and the Culture of Street Art

Take part in Porto's thriving street art scene by going on a street art tour and becoming acquainted with the city's graffiti culture. Join a tour led by skilled neighborhood artists who will show you the secret spots and thriving communities where street art thrives. Learn about the vibrant murals, intricate stencils, and provocative graffiti that decorate the city's walls and turn them into outdoor art exhibits. Discover the creative minds behind the pieces, their sources of inspiration, and the societal themes they hope to portray. The street art movement in Porto is a tribute to the influence of art in public areas and a reflection of the city's creative spirit.

Craftsmanship and Artisan Workshops

Visit artisan studios to learn about Porto's long history of workmanship and to see the exacting methods that go into making the city's finest handcrafted goods. Discover the world of azulejo tile manufacturing, where talented craftspeople use age-old techniques to produce magnificent tiles. Visit the studios of professional artisans who specialize in producing leather, metal, or wood products to see how their deft hands turn unfinished materials into stunning finished products. Attend seminars where you may pick up traditional skills and produce your original artwork. You may fully appreciate the skill and tenacity of the artisans who uphold these centuries-old traditions by immersing yourself in Porto's artisan workshops.

The vibrant art and design culture in Porto will capture the attention of fans. Explore the cutting-edge creations of regional and worldwide artists at contemporary art galleries and shows. Explore design neighborhoods and studios to locate one-of-a-kind items and get a close-up look at the creative processes. Join street art excursions to experience the intriguing graffiti that graces the city's walls and embrace the thriving street art culture. By visiting artisan studios, you may become fully immersed in the world of craftsmanship and learn about the painstaking processes needed to make unique handcrafted items. Your creativity will be stimulated and inspired by Porto's art and design scene, allowing you to interact with the city's diverse cultural manifestations and depart with a greater understanding of its artistic past.

Chapter 20: Goodbye, Porto

Your Experience in Porto: Some Thoughts

Consider the events and memories you have made as your stay in Porto comes to an end. Consider the sights, tastes, and awe-inspiring experiences that have impacted your heart. Also, consider the flavors you have experienced. Consider the welcoming nature of the people there, the bustling vitality of the city, and the rich cultural legacy that pervades every nook and cranny. Think about the profound impact Porto has had on your life and the wider perspective it has given you. Accept the knowledge and understanding you got during your time in Porto and keep them close to your heart as you move on in life.

Souvenirs and Mementos for Preserving Memories

As you say goodbye to Porto, think about bringing home keepsakes and memorabilia to keep your memories alive. Pick items that perfectly capture your time in Porto and make you happy every time you see them. Perhaps you fell in love with a locally produced work of art, a bottle of Port wine to enjoy at home, or a handcrafted piece of azulejo tile. You might also record your favorite memories, sketches, and ideas about your

Porto journey in a travel diary. Your choice of memories will act as a physical memory of the happiness, beauty, and inspiration you experienced in Porto.

Making Plans for Your Next Trip to Porto

Even if it's time to say goodbye to Porto for the time being, let the city linger in your thoughts and begin organizing your next trip. Think about the locations you missed or the activities you want to experience again. Every time a visitor comes to Porto, they find something new about the city. Perhaps you long to uncover hidden gems, go further afield, or learn more about Porto's thriving art and design scene. By planning your next schedule using the knowledge you've gained from your previous trip, you can make sure that your next trip to Porto is even more magical and exciting.

Bidding Farewell to the Magical City

Since Porto has surely left an impression on your spirit, saying goodbye might be difficult. Spend a minute saying goodbye to the charming city that has won your heart. The renowned Dom Luis Bridge and the charming Ribeira neighborhood may be seen one more time from a calm location beside the Douro River. Take one last moment to take in the sights, sounds, and feel of the city. Describe how grateful you are for the encounters and memories you have had while visiting Porto. Carry the warmth and beauty of Porto with you as you say farewell, knowing that its spirit will always be with you as you navigate life.

Keep your memories alive as you reflect on your time in Porto by collecting special keepsakes and mementos. Plan your next trip now that you are aware that Porto is looking forward to seeing you again. Carry with you the love, inspiration, and appreciation that Porto has given you as you bid adieu to the beautiful city. Porto, I'll miss you till our next encounter.

Bonus Section

When in Porto, Engage in These 20 Special Activities

1. Climb the Clérigos Tower: In the heart of the city, next to the Clérigos Church, lies the Torre dos Clérigos. Take in the expansive views of Porto from the summit.

2. Investigate Livraria Lello: Learn about one of the most stunning bookshops on earth, Livraria Lello. It is near the Clérigos Tower on Rua das Carmelitas.

3. Take a stroll around the Ribeira District: In the heart of the city, in the historic district of Ribeira, which is located along the Douro River, take a stroll through the district's vibrant streets.

Visit the So Bento Train Station, which is in the center of Porto, and behold the magnificent azulejo (Portuguese ceramic tiles).

5. Sample Port Wine at Vila Nova de Gaia: Head over the Dom Luis I Bridge to Vila Nova de Gaia and stop by one of the several Port Wine cellars, such as Taylor's, Sandeman, or Graham's.

6. Take a boat excursion on the Douro River: From the Ribeira District, take a picturesque boat cruise down the Douro River to see Porto from a new angle.

7. Explore the Palácio da Bolsa: Learn about this beautiful structure from the 19th century and take in its luxurious interiors. It is located on Rua Ferreira Borges, close to Ribeira.

Visit the Sé do Porto, the city's cathedral, which is located in the city's old district. Discover its lovely cloisters and take in the sweeping views from the terrace.

9. Explore the Casa da Musica: The Casa da Musica is a cutting-edge performance venue located in the Boavista neighborhood. Immerse yourself in music there. For concerts and events, consult their calendar.

10. Discover Foz do Douro: Travel to the seaside community of Foz do Douro, which is where the Douro River and the Atlantic Ocean converge. Take advantage of the beaches, stroll the promenade, and unwind on the terraces.

11. Visit the Serralves Foundation: The Serralves Foundation, situated in the Parque de Serralves, in the western region of Porto, is home to a museum of modern art and lovely gardens.

12. trip the tram: Board tram line 1, often known as "Electrico," for a delightful and nostalgic trip across the city that passes past storied areas like Massarelos and Batalha.

13. Wander around the Crystal Palace Gardens: The Crystal Palace is a lovely garden complex that is located on a mountaintop in the Miragaia district. Admire the breathtaking scenery.

Visit the Mercado do Bolhao to take in the bustling ambiance of this historic market in Porto. Discover the vibrant kiosks selling local specialties, meat, and fresh veggies.

15. Explore the Lello Bookstore: Go to this exquisite bookstore, which is renowned for its elaborate architecture and lovely staircase. It is situated next to the Clérigos Tower on Rua das Carmelitas.

16. Take a street art tour: Join a guided tour, like the Porto Street Art Tour, that takes you through the city's most artistic areas to learn more about Porto's thriving street art community.

Visit the Museu Nacional Soares dos Reis in the Cedofeita district, which is close to the Crystal Palace Gardens, to immerse yourself in Portuguese art history.

18. Go on a picnic at Parque da Cidade: Unwind in Parque da Cidade, Porto's biggest urban park, which is close to Matosinhos. Take a stroll, hire a bike, or pack a picnic.

19. Take a day excursion to Guimares: Guimares is a picturesque city located approximately 55 kilometers east of Porto and is a great site to learn about the history of Portugal. Explore its World Heritage-listed historic center.

20. Attend a live football game at Estádio do Drago if you're a lover of the sport. Estádio do Drago is the home field of FC Porto. East of the city is where the stadium is situated.

These events provide a wide variety of experiences that highlight Porto's cultural, historical, and natural grandeur. Have fun exploring this fantastic city!

Best Places to Eat

1. Casa Guedes - Rua dos Caldeireiros 188, 4050-138 Porto
2. Abadia do Porto - Rua da Madeira 222, 4000-330 Porto
3. Cafeína - Rua do Padrão 100, 4150-553 Porto
4. Cantinho do Avillez - Rua Mouzinho da Silveira 166, 4050-416 Porto
5. O Gaveto - Rua Roberto Ivens 826, 4450-249 Matosinhos
6. Adega São Nicolau - Rua de São Nicolau 1, 4050-561 Porto
7. A Sandeira - Rua do Almada 13, 4050-036, Porto
8. Conga - Rua do Bonjardim 314, 4000-118, Porto
9. Vinum - Rua do Agro 141, 4400-281 Vila Nova de Gaia
10. Bacalhau - Rua de Cedofeita 442, 4050-180 Porto
11. O Escondidinho - Rua Passos Manuel 45, 4000-381 Porto
12. Rua - Rua da Escola Normal 149, 4150-171 Porto
13. Yuko - Rua da Picaria 81, 4050-478 Porto
14. Bufete Fase - Rua de Santa Catarina 1147, 4000-447 Porto
15. O Paparico - Rua de Costa Cabral 2343, 4200-232 Porto
16. Vinhas d'Alho - Rua de São Francisco 12, 4050-548 Porto
17. Terra - Travessa de Cedofeita 56, 4050-181 Porto

18. Brick Clérigos - Rua de Santo Ildefonso 16, 4000-469 Porto

19. LSD - Largo de São Domingos 89, 4050-545 Porto

20. Tavi - Rua dos Mercadores 36, 4050-375 Porto

These restaurants offer a variety of culinary experiences, ranging from traditional Portuguese cuisine to international flavors. Enjoy exploring the vibrant food scene in Porto!

Best Local Markets in Porto

1. Mercado do Bolhão - Rua de Fernandes Tomás 506, 4000-214 Porto

2. Mercado do Bom Sucesso - Largo Ferreira Lapa, 4050-253 Porto

3. Mercado da Foz - Rua de Diu, 4150-272 Porto

4. Mercado Temporário do Porto - Largo de São Domingos, 4050-545 Porto

5. Mercado Beira-Rio - Avenida Diogo Leite, 4400-111 Vila Nova de Gaia (Located on the Gaia riverside, across from Porto)

6. Mercado Ferreira Borges - Praça Dom João I, 4050-288 Porto

7. Mercado dos Lavradores - Rua Fernandes Tomás 506, 4000-214 Porto

8. Mercado do Marquês - Rua Álvares Cabral, 4050-040 Porto

9. Mercadinho Biológico do Parque da Cidade - Parque da Cidade, 4100-231 Porto

10. Feira da Vandoma - Praça Conde de Agrolongo, 4300-031 Porto (Open on Saturdays, near the Church of Santo Ildefonso)

These local markets offer a variety of products, including fresh produce, seafood, meat, flowers, local crafts, and much more. They provide an opportunity to experience the vibrant atmosphere of Porto's local market scene while exploring the local culture and flavors.

Best Vegetarian Restaurants in Porto

1. DaTerra - Rua do Bonjardim 136, 4000-115, Porto

2. Essência Restaurante Vegetariano - Rua de Santa Catarina 744, 4000-447 Porto

3. Black Mamba - Rua de Passos Manuel 40, 4000-381 Porto

4. Terra - Travessa de Cedofeita 56, 4050-181 Porto

5. Da Terra Bistrô - Rua de Sá da Bandeira 181, 4000-430 Porto

6. Miss Pavlova - Rua de Ceuta 80, 4050-191 Porto

7. Galeria de Paris - Rua da Galeria de Paris 56, 4050-284 Porto

8. Paladar da Alma - Rua do Rosário 177, 4050-524, Porto

9. Vegana Burgers - Rua de Santa Catarina 808, 4000-446 Porto

10. Lado B - Rua Passos Manuel 190, 4000-382 Porto

These vegetarian restaurants offer a variety of plant-based dishes, including vegan and vegetarian options. They are great choices for those seeking delicious and satisfying vegetarian meals in Porto. Enjoy exploring the vegetarian culinary scene in the city!

Best Bars and Clubs in Porto

1. Galeria de Paris - Rua da Galeria de Paris 56, 4050-284 Porto

2. Plano B - Rua Cândido dos Reis 30, 4050-151 Porto

3. Maus Hábitos - Rua Passos Manuel 178, 4000-382 Porto

4. Base - Praça D. Filipa de Lencastre 45, 4050-259 Porto

5. Café au Lait - Rua do Rosário 177, 4050-524 Porto

6. Casa do Livro - Rua Galerias de Paris 85, 4050-283 Porto

7. Bonaparte Downtown - Rua de Cândido dos Reis 98, 4050-151 Porto

8. Baixa Bar - Rua da Picaria 83, 4050-477 Porto

9. Boca do Lobo - Rua de José Falcão 140, 4050-317 Porto

10. Pitch Club - Avenida da Boavista 2021, 4100-132 Porto

These bars and clubs offer a vibrant nightlife experience in Porto, with a variety of music genres, unique atmospheres, and great drink selections. Enjoy exploring the energetic nightlife scene in the city!

Best Places For A Fancy Dinner In Porto

1. Pedro Lemos - Rua do Padre Luís Cabral 974, 4150-464 Porto
2. Antiqva - Rua de Entre Quintas 220, 4050-240 Porto
3. Casa de Chá da Boa Nova - Avenida da Liberdade 1681, 4450-718 Leça da Palmeira
4. DOP - Rua Ferreira Borges 141, 4050-253 Porto
5. The Yeatman - Rua do Choupelo, 4400-088, Vila Nova de Gaia
6. ODE Porto Wine House - Rua do Dr. Barbosa de Castro 63, 4050-090 Porto
7. Astória - Rua da Alegria 29, 4000-043 Porto
8. LSD - Largo de São Domingos 89, 4050-545 Porto

9. Vinum - Rua do Agro 141, 4400-281 Vila Nova de Gaia
10. Tavi - Rua dos Mercadores 36, 4050-375 Porto

These restaurants offer a luxurious dining experience with high-quality cuisine, elegant ambiance, and impeccable service. Enjoy an exquisite meal in one of these fancy establishments in Porto!

Printed in Great Britain
by Amazon